Blending AI & Brand Strategy

Fast-Tracking Your Authority in a Digital World

Copyright Disclaimer

All material contained in this ebook is protected by United States and international copyright laws. The Author's Journey® reserves exclusive ownership of its intellectual property, including its content, design, and layout.

This ebook may not be reproduced, distributed, transmitted, stored in a retrieval system, uploaded, or stored in any platform or external database, or entered into any information storage or retrieval system, in any form or by any method (electronic, mechanical, photocopying, recording, or otherwise), without The Author's Journey's express prior written consent.

It is also prohibited to share, submit, or use this ebook's content in conjunction with any artificial intelligence tool or software without The Author's Journey's express written consent. Violation of this copyright could result in legal action and enforcement of full penalties under copyright law.

For permissions requests, inquiries, or further information, please contact info@theauthorsjourney.co.

The Author's Journey is the sole owner of the intellectual property rights.

ISBN/SKU:979-8-3304-9875-8

Disclosure Policy for AI-Generated Book Content

This book incorporates content that was partially generated or assisted by artificial intelligence (AI) tools. In the spirit of transparency and ethical use of AI technology, we provide this disclosure to our readers.

Use of AI in this book

1. Content Generation: Some sections of this book were initially drafted or expanded using AI language models. This includes certain paragraphs, bullet points, and content ideas.

2. Editing and Refinement: AI tools were used to assist in editing, proofreading, and refining the content for clarity and coherence.

3. Research Assistance: AI was employed to gather information, statistics, and insights that informed the content of this book.

4. Prompts and Examples: The AI prompts and examples provided in the book were generated with the assistance of AI tools.

Human oversight and contribution

While AI tools were utilized in the creation of this book, it's important to note that:

1. All AI-generated content was reviewed, edited, and approved by Elona Washington.

2. The overall structure, main ideas, and core messages of the book were conceived and developed by human authors.

3. Personal experiences, case studies, and specific insights are based on the author's genuine expertise and experiences.

Commitment to quality and accuracy

We are committed to providing high-quality, accurate, and valuable content to our readers. The use of AI in this book is intended to enhance, not replace, human expertise and creativity. We have taken steps to ensure that all information presented is factual and up-to-date at the time of publication.

Feedback and questions

If you have any questions or concerns about the content of this book or our use of AI in its creation, please contact us at [contact information].

By purchasing and reading this book, you acknowledge and accept this disclosure policy regarding the use of AI-generated content.

Table of Contents

Copyright Disclaimer	3
Disclosure Policy for AI-Generated Book Content	4
Table of Contents	6
AI Tools	7
Introduction	11
Branding in the Digital Age	
Chapter 1	13
Foundations of Personal Branding	
Chapter 2	**18**
AI for Career Development	
Chapter 3	**23**
AI-Powered Content Strategy	
Chapter 4	32
Building Brand Authority with AI	
Chapter 5	**38**
Embracing AI for Brand Strategy Success	
Glossary	**41**
About Elona Washington	**44**

AI Tools

Content Creation and Writing

1. Copy.ai
https://www.copy.ai/
Use for: Generating various types of written content, including blog posts, ad copy, and social media captions.

2. Jasper.ai
https://www.jasper.ai/
Use for: Producing long-form content, blog articles, and marketing copy with customizable brand voice settings.

3. ChatGPT
https://chat.openai.com/
Use for: General content ideation, answering brand-related questions, and brainstorming marketing strategies.

4. Claude
https://www.anthropic.com/
Use for: Advanced language tasks, content generation, and analysis with a focus on safety and ethics.

5. Perplexity AI
https://www.perplexity.ai/

Use for: Quick research, fact-checking, and generating concise answers to complex questions.

Visual Content and Design

6. Canva AI
https://www.canva.com/ai-image-generator/
Use for: Creating visually appealing designs, social media posts, and marketing materials with AI-assisted features.

7. Midjourney
https://www.midjourney.com/
Use for: Creating unique, AI-generated images for branding materials and social media content.

8. DALL-E 2
https://openai.com/dall-e-2/
Use for: Generating custom images from text descriptions for brand visuals and marketing campaigns.

Video and Audio Content

9. Lumen5
https://lumen5.com/
Use for: Automatically converting text-based content into engaging video content for brand storytelling.

10. Synthesia
https://www.synthesia.io/

Use for: Creating AI-powered video content with virtual presenters for brand messaging and training.

11. Otter.ai
https://otter.ai/
Use for: Transcribing and analyzing spoken content, useful for repurposing webinars or podcasts into written brand content.

SEO and Content Optimization

12. Surfer SEO
https://surferseo.com/
Use for: Optimizing content for search engines using AI-driven recommendations.

13. MarketMuse
https://www.marketmuse.com/
Use for: AI-powered content planning and optimization to build topical authority for your brand.

Social Media and Brand Monitoring

14. Hootsuite Insights
https://www.hootsuite.com/products/insights
Use for: AI-powered social media analytics and audience insights to inform branding strategies.

15. BrandMentions
https://brandmentions.com/

Use for: AI-driven brand monitoring and social listening to track brand perception and engagement.

Language and Grammar

16. Grammarly
https://www.grammarly.com/
Use for: Ensuring error-free, professional writing across all brand communications.

17. Wordtune
https://www.wordtune.com/
Use for: Enhancing writing clarity by providing suggestions to rephrase sentences or improve tone.

18. QuillBot
https://quillbot.com/
Use for: Paraphrasing text to enhance clarity or change the writing style while maintaining the original meaning.

Marketing Language Optimization

19. Phrasee
https://phrasee.co/
Use for: Generating and optimizing marketing language for emails, push notifications, and social media posts.

Introduction

Branding in the Digital Age

Branding has undergone a rapid transformation with social media platforms, content marketing, and digital advertising becoming the new battlegrounds for attention and loyalty. This digital age has democratized all industries, allowing individuals and small businesses to compete on a global stage alongside celebrities and corporations.

In this hyper-connected world, a strong brand is no longer a nice-to-have; it's a necessity for survival and growth. This doesn't just apply in business but in personal branding and career growth too. Fortunately, artificial intelligence (AI) is further revolutionizing and leveling the playing field when it comes to how individuals and smaller brands approach and implement brand strategy.

From data analysis and content creation to personalized customer experiences and predictive marketing, AI is empowering smaller brands with the power to connect with their audiences faster and more efficiently. The fusion of human creativity with the speed of AI is opening up new possibilities in brand development and management.

If you're looking to build your brand, it's important to understand how to harness the power of AI effectively. This book is your guide to blending AI and brand strategy, whether you're looking to:

- ★ grow your professional career, or
- ★ build a personal brand as a thought leader.

My year-long journey from a 25-year corporate marketing career to a successful six-figure entrepreneur stands as a testament to the transformative power of AI to revolutionize the approach to branding. I attribute this success to the strategic use of AI in developing my brand and marketing approach. This book is designed to help you achieve similar success.

Chapter 1

Foundations of Personal Branding

Whether you're an inspiring thought leader or seeking to advance your career, you need a strong personal brand to open doors and create opportunities. This chapter will guide you through the process of developing a compelling personal brand by leveraging AI for insights and relevant content.

Discovering your core message

At the heart of every strong personal brand lies a clear, compelling core message. This message should encapsulate your unique value proposition (UVP), reflecting your expertise, passions, and the value you bring to your audience. Let's use an AI-powered approach to help you craft your message.

AI prompt for personal brand development

"As a personal branding expert, help me develop a unique personal brand. Consider my background in [your field], my strengths in [list 2-3 key strengths], and my goal to [your main objective]. Provide a step-by-step guide to crafting a compelling personal brand statement, identifying my target audience, and selecting 2-3 content pillars that align with my expertise and goals."

AI-powered personal SWOT analysis

A personal SWOT (Strengths, Weaknesses, Opportunities, Threats) analysis is a commonly used tool for self-assessment and personal branding. By leveraging AI, we can gain deeper insights and uncover aspects you might not have considered on your own.

AI prompts for personal SWOT analysis

"As a career development expert, conduct a detailed Personal SWOT Analysis for a professional in [YOUR FIELD] with [X YEARS] of experience. Consider my background in [SPECIFIC AREAS OF EXPERTISE], my goal to [YOUR CAREER OBJECTIVE], and the current trends in [YOUR INDUSTRY]. Provide:

1. 5 key Strengths
2. 5 potential Weaknesses
3. 5 Opportunities in the current market
4. 5 potential Threats to their career growth

"For each point, provide a brief explanation of its significance and potential impact on my career.

Also, suggest one actionable step to leverage each Strength and Opportunity, and one step to mitigate each Weakness and Threat."

Leveraging your SWOT analysis

After receiving your AI-generated SWOT Analysis, consider the following steps.

1. Analyze the output critically. Does it accurately reflect your situation? Adjust as necessary.

2. Identify and prioritize the most impactful items in each category.

3. Create an action plan to:
    - ★ Capitalize on your strengths
    - ★ Improve your weaknesses
    - ★ Seize opportunities
    - ★ Mitigate threats

4. Use the insights to refine your personal brand message and positioning.

5. Set goals based on the analysis, then set specific, measurable goals for your personal and professional development.

6. Analyze the output periodically (e.g., monthly, quarterly, or annually) to track your progress and adjust your strategies.

This SWOT analysis is also useful when it comes to outlining your career path as well.

Leveraging AI for audience insights

Now that you've defined your core message, it is time to understand and find your ideal audience. AI can help you gather and analyze the data you need to do so.

AI prompt for audience analysis

"As an AI-powered data analyst, examine my target audience in the [YOUR INDUSTRY] sector.
Provide:

1. Detailed demographic breakdown
2. Top 5 content topics they engage with most
3. Preferred content formats (e.g., blog posts, videos, infographics)
4. Best times and platforms for content distribution
5. Key pain points and interests that my content should address"

Understanding your audience

To position yourself appropriately, it's important to understand their frustrations, desires, and fears. Let's use another AI prompt to gain these insights.

AI prompt for audience analysis

"Act as an expert [YOUR TITLE]. Tell me 10 frustrations, 10 desires, and 10 fears that [TARGET AUDIENCE] experience with [INDUSTRY]. Put it in a table format x-axis 1-10 and y-axis frustrations, desires, and fears."

This AI-generated data provides a wealth of information that you can use to:

1. Tailor your personal brand message to address specific pain points.
2. Create content that resonates with your audience's desires.
3. Develop solutions that alleviate their fears.
4. Position yourself as an expert who understands and can solve their problems.

Chapter 2

AI for Career Development

Artificial Intelligence can be a powerful ally in your career journey, offering personalized insights, identifying skill gaps, and suggesting tailored growth opportunities. Here's how you can harness AI to advance your career.

Skill gap analysis

AI can analyze your current skill set against industry trends and job market demands to identify areas for improvement.

AI prompt for skill gap analysis

"As a career development expert, analyze the current job market for [YOUR PROFESSION] in [YOUR LOCATION/INDUSTRY]. Compare the top 10 most in-demand skills for this role with my current skill set [LIST YOUR SKILLS]. Identify any gaps and suggest specific courses, certifications, or experiences to bridge these gaps. Provide a prioritized list of skills to develop, explaining the potential impact of each on my career prospects."

Career path exploration

AI can also help you explore potential career paths based on your interests, skills, and experience.

AI prompt for career path exploration

"Given my background in [YOUR FIELD] with [X YEARS] of experience and strengths in [LIST 2-3 KEY STRENGTHS], suggest 5 potential career paths I could pursue. For each path, provide:

1. A brief description of the role
2. Required skills and qualifications
3. Potential salary range
4. Growth prospects over the next 5 years
5. One step I can take immediately to move towards this path"

Personal brand enhancement

AI can assist in refining your personal brand to align with your career goals.

AI prompt for personal brand enhancement

"Based on my career goal to become a [TARGET POSITION] in the [INDUSTRY] sector, help me enhance my personal brand. Provide suggestions for:

1. Optimizing my LinkedIn profile (including a compelling headline and summary).
2. Topics for thought leadership content I should create.
3. Professional organizations or networks I should join.
4. Personal brand attributes I should emphasize.
5. A strategy to increase my visibility in my desired field."

Interview preparation

AI can help you prepare for job interviews by simulating common questions and providing feedback.

AI prompt for interview preparation

"Act as an interviewer for the position of [JOB TITLE] at a [COMPANY TYPE]. Ask me 10 challenging interview questions specific to this role and industry. After each of my responses, provide feedback on the strength of my answer and suggest improvements. Include at least 2 behavioral questions and 1 technical question relevant to the role."

Networking strategy

AI can assist in developing a targeted networking strategy to advance your career.

AI prompt for networking strategy

"Develop a networking strategy to advance my career as a [YOUR PROFESSION] looking to move into [TARGET ROLE/INDUSTRY]. Include:

1. 5 types of professionals I should connect with.
2. 3 industry events or conferences I should attend.
3. A template for a networking outreach message.
4. 3 online communities or forums I should join.
5. Tips for maintaining and leveraging my professional network."

Continuous learning plan

AI can help create a personalized learning plan to keep your skills current and competitive.

AI prompt for continuous learning plan

"Create a 6-month continuous learning plan for a [YOUR PROFESSION] looking to stay competitive in the [INDUSTRY] sector. Include:

1. 3 emerging technologies or trends I should focus on.

2. 5 specific skills to develop, with resources for each (e.g., online courses, books, workshops).
3. A weekly schedule balancing work, learning, and personal time.
4. Metrics to track progress and assess the impact on my career.
5. Suggestions for applying new skills in my current role."

By leveraging these AI prompts, you can gain valuable insights and create actionable plans for your career development. Remember to combine AI-generated advice with your own judgment and seek guidance from your manager when making significant career decisions. AI is a tool to augment your decision-making, not replace it entirely.

By following these steps and leveraging AI to generate ideas, you'll be well on your way to building a strong personal brand that resonates with your target audience and helps you achieve your professional goals.

Chapter 3

AI-Powered Content Strategy

In this chapter, we'll explore how to leverage AI to create a robust, effective content strategy that aligns with your brand. AI tools can significantly enhance your content creation process, from ideation to optimization and distribution.

Crafting your content strategy

Now that you have an understanding of your core message and audience insights, it's time to develop a content strategy that will help you stand out and grow your audience. But before diving into specific content ideas, it's crucial to establish overarching themes or pillars that align with your brand's core message and resonate with your target audience. Use the following AI prompt to generate these pillars:

AI prompt for content pillars

"As an AI content strategist, create a list of 5-7 compelling content pillars based on the following inputs:

1. Core Message: [Insert your brand's core message or value proposition]
2. Audience Characteristics:
   - Demographics: [Age range, gender, location, etc.]
   - Psychographics: [Interests, values, lifestyle, pain points]
   - Professional Background: [Industry, job roles, experience level]
3. Brand Voice: [Describe your brand's tone and style, e.g., professional, friendly, innovative]
4. Key Topics: [List 3-5 main topics your brand focuses on]
5. Content Goals: [e.g., educate, inspire, solve problems, entertain]

For each content pillar, provide:

- A catchy title
- A brief description (2-3 sentences)
- How it relates to your core message
- Why it would resonate with your audience
- 2-3 potential subtopics or content ideas within this theme

Ensure that the themes are diverse yet cohesive, aligning with your brand strategy and addressing different aspects of your audience's interests and needs.

AI prompt for content strategy

"Based on my personal brand focused on [your niche] for [target audience], generate 10 engaging social media post ideas, 5 email newsletter topics, and 3 blog post outlines that align with my brand message and resonate with my audience. Ensure the content showcases my expertise in [your field] and addresses common pain points or interests of my target audience."

AI tools for content optimization

Once you understand your audience, AI can help you generate ideas to optimize your content for maximum impact.

AI prompt for content ideation

"Based on the audience analysis for [YOUR INDUSTRY], generate
1. 20 compelling blog post titles
2. 15 social media post concepts
3. 10 video topic ideas
4. 5 potential series or content pillar ideas
Ensure these ideas align with current trends and address the identified audience pain points."

AI prompt for content optimization

"For the blog post titled [INSERT TITLE], provide
1. 5 SEO-optimized headings
2. 10 relevant long-tail keywords to incorporate
3. Ideal word count for maximum SEO impact
4. Suggestions for internal and external links
5. An optimized meta description"

Implementing AI-driven personalization

Personalization can significantly boost engagement with your content. AI can help you tailor your content to individual user preferences and behaviors.

AI prompt for content personalization strategy

"Develop a strategy for personalizing content for my [BUSINESS TYPE] using AI. Include:

1. Types of data to collect for personalization
2. 5 ways to segment the audience
3. Ideas for dynamically adjusting content based on user behavior
4. Suggestions for personalized content recommendations
5. Metrics to measure the effectiveness of personalization"

Balancing AI assistance with human creativity

While AI is a powerful tool, it's essential to maintain the human touch in your content. Here are some tips for striking the right balance:

1. Use AI for research and ideation, but craft the final narrative yourself.
2. Leverage AI for data-driven insights, but interpret them with human intuition.
3. Use AI-generated content as a starting point, then edit and refine it.
4. Always fact-check AI-generated information.

Creating an AI-powered content calendar

An effective content strategy requires consistent publishing. AI can help you create and maintain an optimal content calendar. Go to canva.com for a calendar template then use the prompt below.

AI prompt for content calendar

"Create a 3-month content calendar for my [BUSINESS TYPE]. Include:

1. Optimal posting frequency for each platform

2. Content themes aligned with business goals and audience interests
3. Suggestions for repurposing content across platforms
4. Important dates or events to create content around
5. A mix of content types (e.g., educational, promotional, entertaining)"

Measuring Content Performance with AI

Several AI-powered tools have emerged as game-changers. Let's explore some of the most impactful ones.

1. Canva AI

Canva AI has revolutionized visual content creation, making it accessible to everyone, regardless of design experience.

Key Features
- ★ Magic Design Instantly creates designs based on your content and brand
- ★ Text to Image Generates custom images from text descriptions
- ★ Magic Eraser Removes unwanted elements from images
- ★ Background Remover Automatically removes image backgrounds

AI prompt for Canva AI design

"As a Canva AI expert, provide a step-by-step guide on how to use Canva AI to create a visually appealing social media post for [YOUR BRAND] in the [YOUR INDUSTRY] sector. Include tips on using Magic Design, Text to Image, and color palette selection to ensure brand consistency."

2. Copy.ai

Copy.ai is an AI-powered writing assistant that helps create various types of content, from blog posts to ad copy.

Key Features
- ★ Blog post wizard
- ★ Product description generator
- ★ Social media content creator
- ★ Email subject line generator

AI prompt for Copy.ai content creation

"Acting as a Copy.ai specialist, outline a process for using Copy.ai to create a comprehensive blog post about [YOUR TOPIC] for [YOUR TARGET AUDIENCE]. Include tips on how to use the tool's features to generate an outline, craft compelling headlines, and develop engaging body content while maintaining a consistent brand voice."

3. Jasper.ai

Jasper.ai (formerly Jarvis) is an advanced AI writing tool that can generate long-form content and adapt to specific brand voices.

Key Features
- ★ Long-form assistant
- ★ SEO optimization
- ★ Brand voice customization
- ★ Integration with Surfer SEO

AI prompt for Jasper.ai usage

"As a Jasper.ai expert, provide a detailed guide on how to use Jasper.ai to create a 1500-word article about [YOUR INDUSTRY TREND] that aligns with [YOUR BRAND]'s voice and style. Include tips on using the long-form assistant, optimizing for SEO, and maintaining brand consistency throughout the article."

Ethical Considerations in AI-Powered Content Strategy

As you implement AI in your content strategy, keep these ethical considerations in mind:

1. Disclose the use of AI in content creation when appropriate.

2. Ensure AI-generated content aligns with your brand voice and values.
3. Regularly review AI-generated content for accuracy and bias.
4. Use AI to enhance, not replace, human creativity.

By leveraging AI in these ways, you can create a powerful, data-driven content strategy that resonates with your audience and supports your brand goals. Remember, the most effective content strategies combine the analytical power of AI with human creativity, empathy, and strategic thinking.

Chapter 4

Building Brand Authority with AI

Getting started is the first step; but establishing and maintaining brand authority is crucial for success. AI offers powerful tools and strategies to enhance your brand's credibility, reach, and influence. This chapter explores how to leverage AI to build and solidify your brand authority, while also looking ahead to emerging technologies and strategies for staying adaptable in a rapidly evolving AI landscape.

Leveraging AI for Thought Leadership

AI can significantly enhance your ability to produce high-quality, authoritative content that positions you as a thought leader in your industry. Here's how:

1. Content Research and Ideation - Use AI to analyze trending topics, identify knowledge gaps, and generate unique content ideas that resonate with your audience.

2. Data-Driven Insights - Leverage AI to process vast amounts of data, uncovering valuable insights

that can inform your content strategy and demonstrate your expertise.

3. Content Creation and Optimization - Utilize AI writing assistants to draft articles, reports, and whitepapers, ensuring they're optimized for search engines and reader engagement.

4. Personalized Content Distribution - Implement AI-driven content recommendation systems to deliver the right content to the right audience at the right time.

AI prompt for thought leadership strategy

"As an AI expert in thought leadership, create a comprehensive strategy for establishing [YOUR BRAND] as a thought leader in the [YOUR INDUSTRY] sector. Include:

1. Top 5 content themes that will position us as industry experts.
2. 3 innovative ways to use AI in creating authoritative content.
3. A plan for leveraging AI to identify and engage with key industry influencers.
4. Strategies for using AI to measure and improve our thought leadership impact.
5. Suggestions for AI-powered tools to enhance our content creation and distribution process."

Emerging AI Technologies in Branding

As AI continues to evolve, new technologies are emerging that have the potential to revolutionize branding strategies. Here are some forward-looking AI technologies to watch:

1. Generative AI for Visual Branding - Advanced AI models capable of creating unique, brand-consistent visual content, including logos, marketing materials, and even video content.

2. Emotion - AI Technologies that can detect and respond to human emotions, allowing for more empathetic and emotionally resonant brand interactions.

3. Voice AI and Sonic Branding - As voice interfaces become more prevalent, AI will play a crucial role in developing and maintaining consistent sonic brand identities.

4. Augmented Reality (AR) and AI - The combination of AR and AI will enable more immersive and interactive brand experiences.

5. Quantum Computing in AI - As quantum computing advances, it will enable more complex AI models, potentially revolutionizing data analysis and predictive capabilities for branding.

AI prompt for future AI branding trends

"As a futurist specializing in AI and branding, provide insights on how the following emerging AI technologies might impact branding strategies in the next 5-10 years:

1. Generative AI for visual content
2. Emotion AI
3. Advanced voice AI
4. AR/VR combined with AI
5. Quantum computing in AI

For each technology, suggest potential applications in branding and how they might change current practices."

Adapting to AI Advancements

To remain competitive and maintain brand authority, it's crucial to stay agile and adapt to rapid advancements in AI. Here are strategies to help your brand remain flexible and innovative:

1. Continuous Learning Culture - Foster a culture of continuous learning within your organization, encouraging team members to stay updated on AI advancements.

2. Experimentation and Pilot Programs - Regularly test new AI technologies through small-scale pilot programs before full implementation.

3. Cross-Functional AI Teams - Create cross-functional teams that bring together marketing, IT, and data science expertise to drive AI innovation in your branding efforts.

4. Ethical AI Framework - Develop and regularly update an ethical AI framework to ensure responsible use of AI in your branding strategies.

5. Flexible Technology Stack - Build a flexible, modular technology stack that can easily integrate new AI tools and technologies as they emerge.

6. Partnerships and Collaborations - Form strategic partnerships with AI startups, research institutions, or technology providers to stay at the forefront of AI advancements.

AI prompt for AI adaptation strategy

"As an AI strategy consultant, develop a comprehensive plan for [YOUR BRAND] to stay agile and adapt to rapid AI advancements in the branding space. Include:

1. A framework for evaluating new AI technologies for potential adoption
2. Strategies for upskilling team members in AI-related competencies
3. A roadmap for gradually increasing AI integration in branding processes

4. Risk management strategies for AI implementation
5. Methods for measuring the ROI of AI adoption in branding efforts
6. Suggestions for fostering a culture of innovation and adaptability"

By leveraging current AI technologies and preparing for future advancements, you can build and maintain strong brand authority in an increasingly AI-driven world. Remember, the key is to use AI as a tool to enhance your brand's unique voice and values, not to replace the human elements that make your brand authentic and relatable.

Chapter 5

Embracing AI for Brand Strategy Success

As we conclude this journey through AI-powered brand strategy, it's clear that the fusion of artificial intelligence and personal branding offers unprecedented opportunities for professional growth. By leveraging AI tools and techniques, you can develop a compelling personal brand, create engaging content, and stay ahead in your career.

Key takeaways

1. Foundation Building - Use AI to craft your core message, conduct a personal SWOT analysis, and gain deep insights into your target audience.

2. Career Development - Leverage AI for skill gap analysis, career path exploration, and interview preparation to advance your professional journey.

3. Content Strategy - Employ AI tools to generate ideas, optimize content, and create personalized experiences that resonate with your audience.

4. Tool Mastery - Familiarize yourself with AI-powered tools like Canva AI, Copy.ai, and Jasper.ai to enhance your content creation process.

5. Real-World Application - Learn from case studies of successful AI implementation in branding and marketing strategies.

Staying up-to-date on trends

In the rapidly evolving landscape of AI and branding, staying current is crucial. Here are strategies to keep yourself informed:

1. Follow AI Thought Leaders - Connect with AI experts and influencers on social media platforms like LinkedIn and Twitter.

2. Subscribe to AI Newsletters - Sign up for newsletters from reputable AI companies and research institutions.

3. Attend Virtual Conferences - Participate in online webinars and conferences focused on AI in marketing and branding.

4. Join Online Communities - Engage in discussions on forums like Reddit's r/artificial or AI-focused Slack channels.

5. Experiment Continuously - Regularly test new AI tools and features to understand their potential applications in your branding strategy.

6. Set Up Google Alerts - Create alerts for key terms like "AI in branding" or "AI marketing trends" to receive relevant news articles.

7. Read Industry Reports - Review annual reports from leading consulting firms on AI trends in marketing and branding.

Final thoughts

As you implement your AI-powered branding strategy, remember that consistency and authenticity are key. Your brand should be a genuine reflection of who you are and what you stand for. Use the insights and content ideas generated by AI as a starting point, but always infuse your unique voice and perspective into everything you create.

Personal branding is an ongoing process. Regularly assess the impact of your efforts using analytics tools and audience feedback. Be prepared to evolve your brand as you grow and as your industry changes. The future of branding is here, and it's powered by the harmonious blend of human creativity and artificial intelligence.

Glossary

AI (Artificial Intelligence)
Technological systems that simulate human intelligence to perform tasks such as data analysis, content creation, and personalized customer experiences.

Brand Authority
The level of trust and credibility a brand holds in its industry, often established through consistent, high-quality content and engagement.

Brand Voice
The distinct personality and style of communication that a brand uses across all its content, reflecting its values and mission.

Content Calendar
A schedule that outlines what content will be published and when, helping to ensure consistency and strategic alignment with business goals.

Content Pillars/Themes
Key topics or themes that a brand focuses on to create content for their social media, blogs, and emails.

Core Message
The central idea or value proposition that defines a brand's identity and resonates with its target audience.

Demographic Breakdown
A detailed analysis of a target audience's characteristics, including age, gender, income level, education, and more.

Engagement Metrics
Data points that measure how users interact with content, such as likes, shares, comments, and click-through rates.

Output
In the context of AI and branding, "output" refers to the results generated by an AI system or tool after processing input data.

Personal Brand
The unique combination of skills, experiences, and personality that an individual presents to the world to distinguish themselves professionally.

Personalization
The practice of tailoring content or experiences to individual user preferences based on data analysis.

SEO (Search Engine Optimization)
The process of optimizing content to improve its visibility on search engines, thereby increasing organic traffic.

SWOT Analysis (Strengths, Weaknesses, Opportunities, Threats)
A strategic planning tool used to identify internal strengths and weaknesses as well as external opportunities and threats related to a business or individual.

Thought Leadership
Establishing oneself as an authority in a specific field by sharing insights, knowledge, and innovative ideas through various platforms.

Unique Value Proposition (UVP)
A statement that clearly articulates the distinct benefits and value a brand offers compared to competitors.

About Elona Washington

Elona Washington combines her 25 years of award-winning marketing expertise and passion for empowering voices to help professionals build their brands and write their success stories—both literally and figuratively.

She is a three-time bestselling author and has designed award-winning marketing campaigns for *New York Times* and *USA TODAY* bestselling authors.

In her corporate marketing career, she developed a webinar strategy that resulted in $1 million in sales and routinely exceeded company and industry benchmarks.

As the founder and CEO of The Author's Journey, Elona empowers professionals and aspiring authors to maximize their brand and financial potential through their ventures in authorship.

As a result, clients regularly experience increased brand visibility, significant revenue growth, and transformation into thought leaders in their industries through:

- ★ Strategic brand development and marketing
- ★ Authentic storytelling and content creation
- ★ Publishing expertise and industry insights

Her clients have achieved remarkable success, including:

- ★ Tripling their ROI within months of book publication
- ★ Securing speaking engagements at prestigious events
- ★ Launching successful consulting practices
- ★ Attracting media attention and expanding their influence

A proud alumna of Howard University, Elona holds a Master of Science in Marketing Management from the University of Maryland University College. She is a member of Delta Sigma Theta Sorority, Inc., and resides in Nashville, TN, with her two sons.

Workshop Information

Elona Washington offers a range of specialized workshops tailored for colleges and universities, corporations, and nonprofits.

These interchangeable workshops are designed to provide practical, actionable strategies that participants can immediately implement to elevate their personal and institutional brands in the digital age.

Colleges and universities

For faculty members, she presents:

- ★ Blending AI & Brand Strategy
- ★ Publishing and Promoting Academic Work

Administrators can benefit from:

- ★ Empowering Student Brands: A Strategic Approach for Career Centers

Corporations

- ★ 360-Degree Branding: Everyone's Role Matters

Nonprofits

- ★ Building a Purpose-Driven Brand for Nonprofits and Associations

Speaking & Workshop Opportunities

For those interested in exploring speaking engagements or workshops that further investigate the integration of AI and brand strategy, Elona Washington welcomes inquiries.

Interested parties may reach out to her at inquiries@theauthorsjourney.co.

www.ingramcontent.com/pod-product-compliance
Lightning Source LLC
LaVergne TN
LVHW051926060526
838201LV00062B/4702